Needle Crafts 12

MACHINE

EMBROID

SEARCH PRESS
London & New York

Introduction

This is a creative guide to simple sewing machine techniques. The machine must have a darning or an ordinary foot. If you use a variety of threads or fabrics, or mix machine techniques, your work will soon bear your own style, but you must practice working out designs on your own machine with your own fabrics. This takes patience, but is worthwhile.

Choosing a machine

No particular machine is recommended, but certain features are desirable;

(a) Your machine must be electric and have a swing needle.

(2) A machine need not be expensive: several inexpensive models work well if you look after them.

(3) Avoid a machine with nylon or plastic moving parts.

(4) A machine with a free arm is not so strong as one with a flat bed, but is adequate for ordinary, domestic use.

(5) Make sure the entire spool case, and not just the spool inside it, is removable from the machine. This is necessary for free embroidery and for very thick threads which will not go through the eye of the needle.

(6) Make sure you can lower the teeth or feed dog, or use a cover plate.

(7) The machine must have a reverse feed. This is easier to operate with a separate button than a lever or a dial.

(8) Buy the best machine you can afford.

Understanding your machine

All machines vary in design and working method, especially in the filling of the spool. Only general information is given here, so first read your instruction manual carefully, and keep it with your machine.

Needles

There are two types of sewing machine: precision (which are expensive) and non-precision. There are two types of needle for these two categories of machine and you must know the difference between them.

The precision needle, 705H, has a curved cut-out at the back of the pointed end which allows for extreme accuracy when the needle goes down into the fabric. The other needle, 130, does not have this feature. The 130/705H needle will do for all machines.

Needles are made in different sizes and are numbered: the larger the number, the larger the needle.

Continental needle size	English equivalent
70	10/12
80	14
90	16
100	18

Thread

As a general rule, the thicker the thread, the larger the needle required to take it. When sewing, the finer the fabric, the finer the needle; but a large needle is often used for machine embroidery as it will stand up better to the speed and strain of this type of work.

A 100/18 size needle and Sylko No. 40 are suitable for almost any piece of machine embroidery.

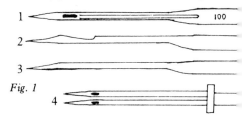

Fig. 1

Fig. 1
(1) *The front view of a needle, showing the groove that runs up the centre for positioning it in the machine.*
(2) *The side view of a precision needle 705H, with the cut-section near the eye.*
(3) *A non-precision needle 130 which will spoil any precision machine.*
(4) *A twin needle. The further apart the two needles are, the more limited is the swing that can be used.*

2

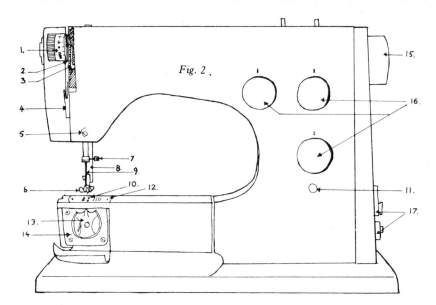

Fig. 2

Fig. 2
1) Upper thread tension dial. This is usually situated near the top thread.
2) Thread tension discs. These pinch together, holding the thread.
3) Thread take-up lever. This moves up and down as you machine.
4) Thread guide.
5) Front thread guide.
6) Presser foot.
7) Needle clamp screw. Make sure that this is tight, and the needle is well in.
8) Presser bar. This brings the foot up and down.
9) Needle. Make sure that the needle is correct, and the groove is the right way round.
10) Feed dog. Moves the fabric through.
11) Knob. This lowers the feed dog, when using the darning foot or sewing free embroidery (not always located here).
12) Needle plate.
13) Spool or bobbin case.
14) Plate. This holds the spool case in position and is removed when the machine jams up.
15) Hand wheel.

(16) Three dials. These set the stitch length, stitch width and various patterns. They might be arranged differently on other machines.
(17) Thread guide and bobbin winding spindle. This is sometimes located on top of the machine.

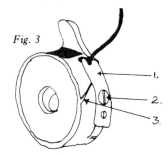

Fig. 3

Fig. 3
The side of a typical spool case:
(1) Flat metal tension spring.
(2) Large screw used to alter the tension.
(3) Slit through which the thread passes before emerging from under the tension spring.

Tension

The tension of the top thread is usually indicated in small numbers on a dial, marked 0–8 (or 0–9) as illustrated in fig. 2. The thread must pass through this mechanism. The higher the number, the tighter the tension and the closer the discs grip the thread. The thread operates only when the presser foot is down in the sewing position.

Spool case

This must be removable, as indicated in fig 3. Spool cases vary slightly: look in your instruction manual to see how to thread the spool and put it into the machine properly. All spool cases have a small, flat sprung piece of metal on the side, attached by one or two screws. There is always a slit into which the spool thread passes, before it slides underneath the spring.

Spool tension

If there are two small screws to hold the tension spring to the outside of the spool, then alter the larger of these. Turn it clockwise to tighten the thread, and anti-clockwise to loosen it. It is a very sensitive mechanism; make only fine adjustments. Think of the head of the screw as the face of a clock: turn the screw 'five minutes' at a time and then try the stitch. Repeat until the tension is correct.

Combined tensions

The top and bottom tensions must be equal for normal work. If you use two different colours you can easily see if the threads interlock within the thickness of the fabric. If one thread remains flat on the fabric surface, it is too tight and should be loosened to avoid puckering the fabric. Because machines vary, tension numbers cannot be quoted, so you must decide the best working tensions for your machine. Tensions vary on different fabrics, so always try out the stitch on a sample of the same fabric and the same number of layers as you will use.

When you use zig-zag, the thread will tighten as it is dragged from side to side. Sometimes you need

only loosen the top tension, while at other times especially when neatening the edges of seams, yo must loosen the bottom tension as well. Always adjus only 'five minutes' at one time on the lower tensio screw.

Fabrics

Cottons and fine wools are the easiest fabrics to wor on because they rarely pucker and can be pressed o the wrong side afterwards to improve the look of th work. Different fabrics used together are less easy t work on, and very fine lawns and organzas are diffi cult to manage because they slip more easily unde the machine foot, and pucker.

A smooth start to sewing

To bring the spool thread up through the hole, hol the needle thread in your fingers and make one com plete stitch by turning the machine drive-wheel wit your other hand. Pull the needle thread sideways bring up the looped spool thread, and then draw ou both threads and place them at the back of the ma chine. Place the fabric under the presser-foot an either hold the two thread ends, or place your fing over where they are. Put the needle into the fabri then put the presser foot down and turn the driv wheel towards you by hand. Make one or two stitch and then put your foot down on the motor control take up the drive. Let go of the threads and concen trate on guiding the fabric.

As a general rule, always start the machine by han and then let the motor drive take over.

Threads

These threads are for use on top of the machine ar will pass through the eye of the needle:

page 5:
This is an effective way of using a large printed fabric, applied very simply in squares, to build up more interest. Lin of satin stitch and automatic patterns, in colours that blend with the print, connect the squares in a border design.

Sylko no. 40 is suitable for most sewing. It is bold and has a smooth, satin finish which is ideal for satin stitch zig-zag.

Sylko no. 50 is a little finer than Sylko no. 40.

Machine embroidery threads nos. 30/40/50 are very fine and soft and break easily unless you are careful. Use them only when you want a very fine effect.

Drima stretches and is very difficult to use in machine embroidery.

Gütermann is slightly thinner and duller than Sylko but looks good.

Buttonhole twist is top stitching thread. It is thicker and much bolder, so a large 100–18 needle and a slightly looser top tension are necessary. Use Sylko underneath.

Cotton perlé no. 8 and fine crochet threads are soft and about as thick as buttonhole twist. Use a large needle. 100–18, and loosen the top tension. Use Sylko underneath.

Most other threads are too thick to go through the eye of the needle and need to be wound on to the spool, so you must work upside-down. See page 18.

Feet

Several feet are available. The basic types for general work are:

See-through foot. A clear, plastic foot is useful as you can watch the fabric when sewing difficult curves or lines that close together.

Appliqué zig-zag foot. Look underneath a foot to find one with a wide, cut-out groove that sometimes tapers off at the back. This is for satin stitch and makes the wide bulk slide easily under the foot. It can be used for general work too.

Cording foot. This foot has a small, arched, tunnel-like groove underneath through which a cord or thick wool thread can pass and stay in place as you sew. Cording feet with two or more grooves cut underneath are available. These are awkward to use if you only want to stitch down one thread, but are ideal for sewing down two or more threads at once.

Darning foot. This foot contains a sprung mechanism

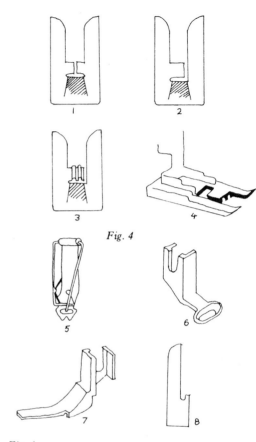

Fig. 4

Fig. 4

(1) and (2) show the underside of basic zig-zag feet, where t. grooves are cut deeper to take the thickness of stitching.

(3) and (4) show a cording foot with two grooves from the si and underneath. The archway grooves are for applying cord wool thread.

(5) and (6) are two kinds of darning foot. There is a spring mechanism either in the machine itself, or outside on the foot as shown.

(7) and (8) show a one-sided zipper foot from the side and from below.

d moves up and down with the needle, enabling
ou to move the fabric and machine it in any
irection.
ip foot. This is a one-sided foot and is useful if you
ant to machine beside a thicker piece of fabric.

All other machine feet are for general dressmaking
chniques and are not appropriate for embroidery.
ou can vary foot pressure to suit the thickness of
bric: follow the instructions in your manual. When
arting machine embroidery, avoid colour contrasts
d concentrate on the effects of fabric textures
ainst one another. Contrasting textures, such as
tin ribbon on denim, or velvet on wool or lace on
tton, together with interesting threads and stitches,
ve an effect as bold as any colour contrast. Use bold
lour variations and contrasts in embroidery when
u are more confident and experienced.

raight and zig-zag stitch
ou can use these two stitches separately, but if you
e them together, they enhance one another.

raight stitch
ith an all-purpose thread (such as Sylko no. 40) on
p and on the spool, and normal tension, straight
tch is the usual stitch for seaming. As a decoration,
is quite fine and needs several lines to make an
pact. Use buttonhole thread for a thicker line and
lko perlé no. 8 for the thickest (see Threads, page

Ribbon and lace are stitched with straight or small
en zig-zag stitches. Wash all ribbon and lace before
plying, unless they are made of nylon. Pin and tack
refully before machining. Cut shapes which do not
y, such as leather or felt, without a turning and
ply with a straight stitch. Do not wash them.
If your machine will only do a straight stitch, then
rk an applied fabric shape like a patch, provided
is a simple shape. Press turnings to the wrong side
the shape before tacking in position, then machine
se to the folded edge with a straight stitch and
tching thread. Work lines of straight stitches either

straight, wavy or even in crossed directions on a plain
fabric, to make it more interesting. Tucks hold a
crease in a piece of fabric, and are stitched a small
distance away from the folded edge, with a straight
stitch or zig-zag line. A tuck must be straight and
follow the weave.

As tucks need extra fabric, they are stitched before
any other work, and before the garment pattern or
article shape is laid over the material. Work on an
area of fabric before cutting it out. Fold and iron each
tuck before machining. For extreme accuracy, particularly if the weave of your fabric is prominent, pull
out a thread from the fabric, exactly on the line of
the fold.

Reverse feed
Try using reverse feed while you are stitching, so that
you can guide your fabric to produce textures and
angular lines. To cover the fabric, move the material
slightly sideways to prevent stitching over the same
place twice. If a large sideways movement is required,
use the darning foot (see page 22).

page 8:
*Quilt for a child's cot 762 mm × 1.01 m (30 × 40 in). The
design is based on a photograph of a house and garden, seen
through a half-curtained window. It is made of cotton, quilted
with courtelle wadding, and machined with straight stitch and
zig-zag with Sylko no. 40 thread. Each strip is quilted
separately, after the appliqué shapes for the house and garden
are completed (Christine Vick).*

page 9:
*Cushion. This basket of flowers is applied with satin stitch in
Sylko no. 40 thread. The fabrics are backed with a thin layer
of iron-on stiffening, because they are placed at odd angles
that don't match the grain of the background. Stiffening
prevents the shapes wrinkling (Phillippa Kendall).*

Zig-Zag

Satin stitch (close zig-zag). The larger the zig-zag number, the wider the stitch. If the stitch length is long, it will be very open. As you reduce the length of stitch, the zig-zag closes until it becomes a satin stitch, when the length of the stitch will be about 0.5.

Satin stitch can be used as a line by itself, or to fasten one piece of fabric around the edge to another. Apply some fabrics with an open zig-zag, if they do not fray easily, or if you wish to cover the edge with hand embroidery.

Method

Set the machine to do satin stitch: length short, width wide (on some machines, length 0.5, width 4). This is necessary to give a smooth look to the right side of the stitch. The spool thread must be a little tighter and stay underneath the fabric, but do not tighten it – you could pucker the fabric. Tissue, or possibly greaseproof paper placed underneath, helps to keep thinner and softer fabrics flat.

For an angular, geometric design, try altering the width of a stitch when you turn a corner, by leaving the needle in the material, lifting the presser foot, and changing width. Turning the needle on the inside rather than the outside of a corner gives a different look.

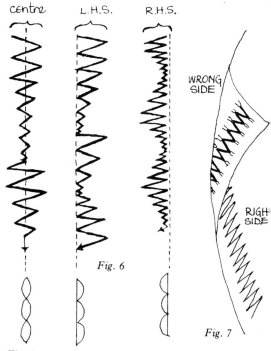

Fig. 6

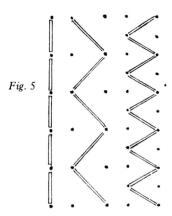

Fig. 5

Fig. 5
Three rows of stitching show how to bring a zig-zag closer together. The row on the left is straight stitch (4). The centre row has the same length stitch as the left-hand row, but with a wide zig-zag (about 4/4). The row on the right has a shorter stitch length with wide zig-zag (above 2/4).

Fig. 6
If your machine has a needle position control, it will make a great deal of difference when altering the width of a zig-zag. Patterns that look automatic are achieved by using this facility.

Fig. 7
This shows a good tension for a perfect satin stitch used as surface decoration. Tension must be slightly looser on top, so that the spool thread stays underneath the fabric.

Altering width

Try altering the width of the stitch as you work, first in straight lines, then in a curve. You will not damage the machine if you do this while the machine is running. It is only when the needle is stationary in the fabric that you must not alter the width. If the needle position is in the middle of the stitch, it will change width equally on both sides. If the needle position is on the left or right, it will remain level on that side.

Altering length

You can alter the length of the stitch while you work, to bring the stitches closer or further apart, but the width remains the same. You can alter either the width or the length, but not both at the same time.

Wrong side

The uneven tension on the wrong side of a zig-zag line can give very interesting effects, especially if two colours have been used. Try turning the fabric over to bring the wrong side on to the top, so that it can be used next to a plain satin stitch.

) Satin stitch changing width as each corner is turned. There also a line of straight stitch with perlé no. 5 thread through le A or B in the spool case (see fig. 12).

) Satin stitch, showing the right and wrong side, and the sult of altering the stitch length during machining.

) Satin stitch, done with the needle in the centre position nd altering the stitch width during machining.

) Zig-zag stitch, sewn slightly open and using the reverse ed to overlap the stitches. Add the beads later.

) Felt and wool applied with satin stitch in Sylko no. 40 read. The wool is couched on with a small, open zig-zag itch. Add the beads later. This makes a good belt (Pat hillpott).

page 12:
Small bags enhanced with very careful appliqué, and machined with several widths of satin stitch in Sylko no. 40 thread. Notice the care taken in sewing the curves. The bag flaps are lined and turned inside out (Phillippa Kendall).

page 13:
Single flower cushion. This shows the use of thicker perlé no. 8 thread through the needle, for open zig-zag and satin stitch. The taper up to the point of each petal is done with the needle position on the RHS (see fig. 6). The stamens between the petals are worked by using the reverse feed to go back over the same place, and then narrowing off to a straight stitch. The centre has lines of couched wool, and lastly, some French knots are added by hand. The edge is log cabin patchwork (Pat Phillpott).

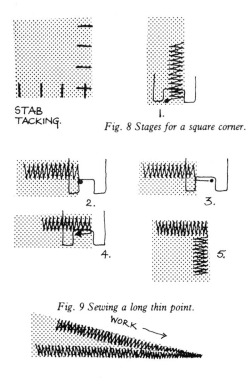

STAB
TACKING.

Fig. 8 Stages for a square corner.

1.

2.

3.

4.

5.

Fig. 9 Sewing a long thin point.

Fig. 10 Stitching ribbon to a curve.

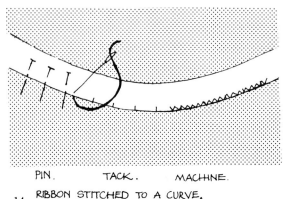

WORK →

PIN.   TACK.   MACHINE.

RIBBON STITCHED TO A CURVE.

Appliqué

Cut the shape exactly to the finished size, keeping the warp or weft threads in the same direction as on the background material. Tack the shape to the background, using the thread colour you will machine with. Instead of a running stitch, use small stab-tacks that go from the edge of the shape inwards, as these stitches secure the fabric more firmly and the machining covers them. Stitch the zig-zag line completely on the shape, and not half on the background material.

Corners

Try not to overlap the zig-zag on the corners; the following method will help to avoid this.

Machine to the corner and stop with the needle on the left-hand side and in the fabric. Lift the presser foot and turn the corner. Lower the foot, so that it is now off the shape. Turn the drive wheel *by hand* so that the needle nearly makes a stitch, away from the shape. Gently lift the presser foot and slide the shape back into place. Lower the presser foot, continue to zig-zag, and it will be in the correct position to work to the next corner.

Curved edges

Work a smooth, even curve by stopping the machine regularly, with the needle on the outer edge of curve. Lift the presser foot, move the shape gently into line again and continue sewing. With tight curves, you must do this every few stitches. The zig-zag will then overlap regularly towards the inner curve.

Points

To sew a long, thin, pointed shape, put the needle position to the right-hand side and narrow off the zig-zag as you approach the point of the shape where two wide zig-zags begin to overlap. Sew back from the tip of the point, overlapping the zig-zags right at the narrow end of the point. Gradually increase the width until the full width of stitch is achieved. The straightest edge must stay on the outside of the shape.

Thread types

Coton à broder. An embroidery cotton used like perlé no. 8.

Crêpe chunky knitting wool. Firm: good for couching on top.

Crewel embroidery wool. Use it in the spool, through holes B or C on the spool case (*see page 18*).

Crochet cotton. As thick as perlé no. 3, but looks like a firm cord. Use it in the spool, or couch on top.

Double knitting wool. Not as easy to use as crêpe wool; it is used in the spool or for couching.

Machine embroidery cotton. This is very much thinner than the Sylko.

Perlé no. 3. Available only in skeins, and used like wool.

Perlé no. 5. For use in the spool with loose or very loose tension (through holes A or B).

Perlé no. 8. For use in the spool, with a normal or loose tension (through hole B on the spool case), through 100 needle (*see fig. 12*).

Rayon crochet thread. This is very slippery and difficult to use. Use it in the spool and pass it through the tension spring.

Soft chunky knitting wool. Used for couching with a wide zig-zag stitch.

Soft embroidery cotton. Used like wool.

Sylko no. 40. Standard machine thread used for nearly all machining.

Tapestry wool. This is often too fluffy for machine use, but can be couched on top.

Textured loopy thread. This is too thick for the spool and must be hand-couched, as it varies in thickness.

Thick crochet cotton. More readily available than perlé no. 3. Use like wool.

Thick machine thread. Used through a needle as for ordinary sewing.

Tricel crêpe double knitting wool. Good on the spool or for couching.

Above, right:
Fig. 11 Blouse or dress using appliqué leaves, satin stitch flowers, and trailing stems of straight stitch in thicker thread.

Fig. 11

page 16:
Green sample. This work is very practical on autumn or winter clothing, or soft furnishing. Knitting wool and stranded cotton are used for a straight stitch through hole B on the spool case (see fig. 12). Other wool threads are couched on top with an open zig-zag stitch (Christine Vick).

page 17:
Pink sample. Worked on a printed fabric with lines of satin stitch in Sylko no. 40 thread, and perlé no. 5 thread for a straight stitch through hole C on the spool case (see fig. 12). The loopy line is produced by having no tension on the thread. The beads have been added afterwards (Pat Phillpott).

16

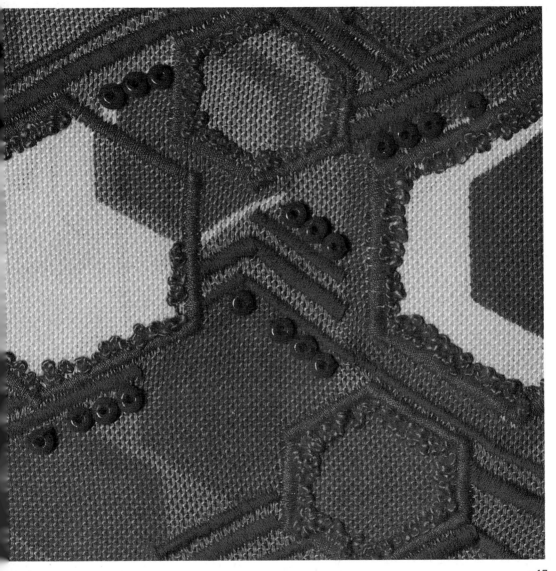

Ribbons

Apply velvet ribbon with a small zig-zag stitch going off the edge. To hold it in place, use a stab-tack that need not be unpicked afterwards. Use the same cotton for tacking and machining. When attaching a straight ribbon round a curved hemline, pin and stitch the lower, larger curve first, then ease the ribbon to the inner curve. Pin, tack and stitch this edge afterwards.

Thick threads, stitched on top, working right-side up

To apply one strand of very thick wool, or two thinner pieces together, adjust the machine to wide-open zig-zag stitch. Use Sylko no. 40 on top and on the spool. Slide the wool up through the slit in the presser foot so that it comes up through the hole in the foot. Put the presser foot down and machine. Guide the wool carefully as you stitch, and be careful not to pull on it.

Thick threads on the spool, working right-side down

As you are likely to use threads thicker than the ordinary sewing thread (Sylko no. 40), it is advisable to buy an extra spool case for embroidery use alone. Then you can alter the tension screw as much as you wish, or remove the whole tension spring without interfering with the tension for your ordinary dressmaking.

An effective way of producing a thick, woolly look is a wind crêpe knitting wool, thick embroidery or crochet threads on the spool. Hold the spool as shown in fig. 14 and put the end of the thread up through the large gap, after the end of the tension spring. Drop the spool in, check that the thick thread flows easily, and place it in the machine. Use Sylko no. 40 on top with normal tension. Try it out first; make a large, straight stitch and then use a wide-open zig-zag.

The loose tension is used up on the zig-zag, and it will look like a woolly rick-rack braid. Remember to turn fabric right-side down, and make sure the two threads are well out to the back of the machine. Place your finger over them and machine in the usual way. The thick thread will stay on the underside.

This stitching looks very good on wool and heavie fabrics for winter wear.

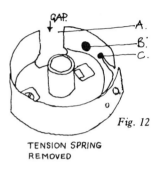

Fig. 12

TENSION SPRING REMOVED

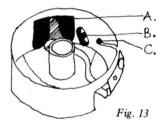

Fig. 13

Figs. 12 and 13
The two basic shapes of spool case, showing the three holes f *the spool thread:*
Hole A is the large gap for wools and thick threads.
Hole B is at the end of the tension spring, and is for perlé n *5 and threads of similar thickness.*
Hole C is for normal tension. If you remove the tension sprin *altogether, this hole can be used for thicker threads, to keep* *more even tension.*
The two larger holes, A and B allow the thread to come out *loose and loop on a straight or narrow zig-zag stitch. Some* *machines loop more than others.*

18

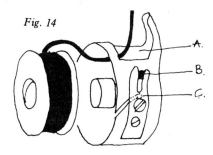

Fig. 14

A.
B.
C.

Fig. 14
Threading wool on a spool.

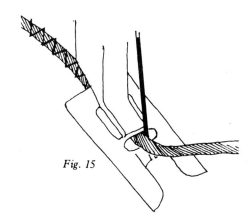

Fig. 15

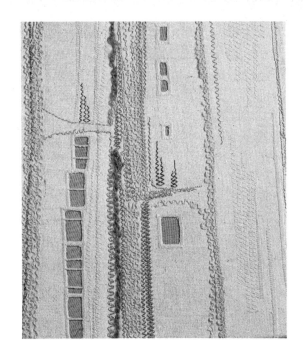

Cream-coloured sample worked for a lampshade. The cream-coloured wool passes through hole A in the spool case for a straight stitch. The other threads pass through hole B or C in the spool case to give a zig-zag stitch of different width and density. The holes in the finished work are cut after completing the zig-zag stitching (Christine Vick).

Fig. 15
Couching down a very thick wool or braid with a wide zig-zag stitch. Pull the thick thread up through the foot before you start. Either one thick or two thin threads side by side, work best.

page 20:
Evening bag worked on pink silk. The design is taken from a photograph of sea and rocks. All the stitching is worked with thicker crochet and perlé cotton threads, passing through hole A or B to give a looser effect. Woollen French knots are added in one area (Louise Whitehurst).

Fig. 16
Make seams more interesting with thicker stitching and automatic patterns.

Below left:
Create a new fabric by co-ordinating with a plain one (Pat Phillpott).

Below right:
A section from the front of a child's cotton dress. The stitching uses a perfect satin stitch and an automatic pattern in character with the applied broderie anglaise (Pat Phillpott).

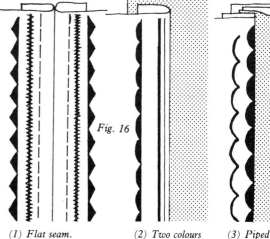

Fig. 16

(1) Flat seam.　　(2) Two colours on either side of a seam.　　(3) Piped seam.

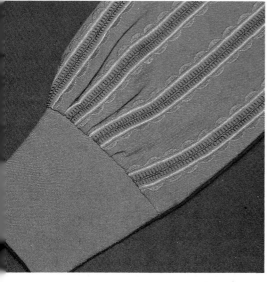

21

Using a darning foot

Try out all your threads on top and on the spool, but this time place the darning foot on the machine. This allows you to move the fabric in any direction and work more intricate and curly designs. Read your instruction manual to check how to lower the teeth or fix a plate over them. Put the presser foot lever down before you begin, as this engages the top tension. Start sewing with the needle in the fabric, and the two thread ends to the back with a finger over them. Start the machine with your right hand, and then sew as usual, guiding the fabric with both hands.

Remember that the speed at which you move the fabric determines the length of the stitch, because you have lowered the teeth. Move the fabric smoothly, and if you wish to work corners or points in the design, pause at that point, and then move on.

Try moving the fabric sideways, as well as in circles or curves. Doodle a free pattern, then doodle a border and try combining this with other formal stitches in your design. You may find that the tension needs to be looser.

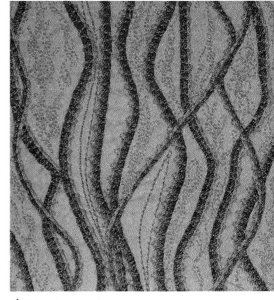

above:
An all-over texture made with couched threads and the multiple couching foot. The background is straight stitch using the quick reverse, and three step zig-zag stitch. (Hazel Chapman).

below:
An edging that combines thick perlé no. 5 worked upside-down with wavy lines in Sylko no. 40 using the darning foot. (Pat Phillpott).

utomatic patterns

very machine produces these differently, so consult
our instruction manual first. The important point is
to turn the zig-zag into a good satin stitch that is
ightly looser on top. Automatic patterns look par-
cularly pretty when used with striped materials. Do
ot space every row evenly, but use different widths
nd threads, leaving some larger spaces between rows.
ucks and lace are very effective when used with
ese patterns.

Automatic patterns are useful for decorating seams,
r as edgings with binding or piping. Do not put too
any different patterns together; try to select those
milar in character.

sing a twin needle

win and triple needles are available, but check that
ey are right for your machine (see fig. 1).

Thread up, with Sylko no. 40, using two threads
top of the machine, one going through each needle,
d with the same thread on the spool.

For a flat effect, loosen the spool as the thread must
g-zag to and fro to catch each needle.

For a quilted, Italian effect, tighten the spool. This
ings the stitches in towards each other, pushing the
bric up between them and giving it a stuffed ap-
arance. This is particularly effective when quilting
clothes with a continuous layer of wadding under
e fabric. You need not back the fabric, provided
e article is lined afterwards. Try using two different
loured threads, or thicker machine thread, which
ust be in both needles. Work slowly as this is tricky
handle.

Automatic patterns, both straight stitch and zig-
g, can be machined with a twin needle. Zig-zag
tch must be set to *half* the usual width as the
achine produces two at a time. If you forget to do
is, the needle goes down straight into the presser
ot and breaks.

above:
Part of a yoke for a blouse made with automatic patterns and tucks worked in one colour (Pat Phillpott).

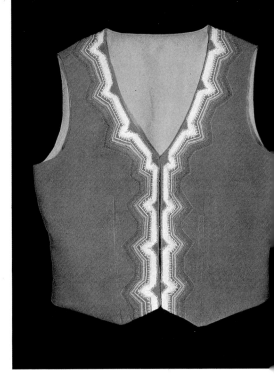

above:
This waistcoat has been washed several times without damaging the embroidery. A twin needle is used with small automatic patterns, and a blind hemming stitch. Sylko no. 40 thread is used throughout (Helen Sant).

left:
Part of a border showing straight ribbon folded to create a geometric pattern. The twin needle is used as well (Helen Sant).

page 25:
This quilting is worked with a twin needle and a straight stitch. Only two layers are worked, the top fabric and the wadding which is lined after machining. The spool tension is tightened slightly to give a ridged look to the line effect (Pat Phillpott).

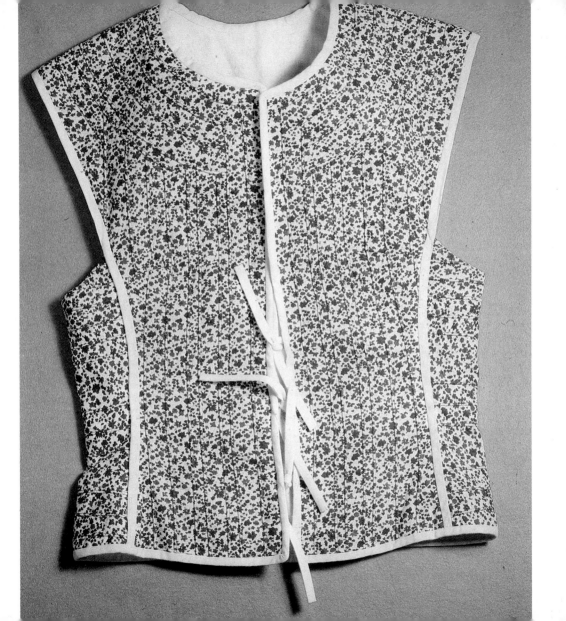

Quilting

Quilting is a sewing technique where padding is enclosed between two layers of fabric (see *Quilting* in the Needle Crafts series). It is very easily and effectively done on a machine. The simplest method is to use a flat layer of terylene wadding. A backing layer is often used but this can be left out. Tack the top fabric and wadding together with crossed lines of tacking, forming squares approximately 5cm (2in) across. A design can be drawn on the back of the fabric (if an additional backing layer is used), and stitched upside-down. Otherwise, tack the design on the right side and machine the same side. Use straight stitch, satin stitch, open zig-zag or even an automatic pattern, and sew with a normal tension. Press the fabric down with a needle to prevent puckering as it approaches the presser foot. You can use a twin needle.

You can machine two layers of fabric together, and then stuff wadding in between them from the back. This works well for shapes and lines and is known as 'Trapunto quilting'. Cut a slit, following the weft or warp, in the backing fabric and insert washable stuffing for household or fashion use. Sew up with a fishbone stitch.

For quilted Italian lines, simply thread wool through from the back with a large needle, coming out at the back where necessary, and going in again at the same place, moving along the line. If a transparent fabric is used on top, then coloured stuffing can be used.

You can also place a piece of coloured fabric between two layers of material and machine round the edge. This is known as shadow quilting. You can use straight stitch or automatic patterns round the edges of shapes, and if you work on lawn, organdy or chiffon, they are most effective for fashion purposes. The darning foot is useful for curves and textures, between and over these shapes.

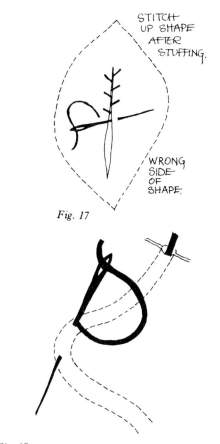

Fig. 17

Fig. 17
Italian quilting. Wool is threaded through between two lines of machining.

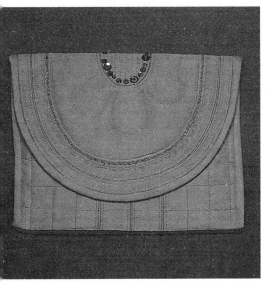

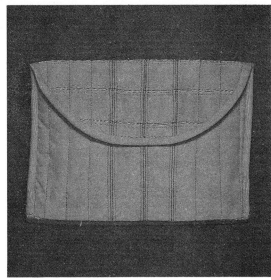

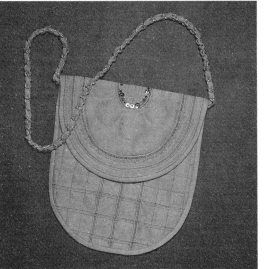

Three quilted evening bags. Terylene wadding is placed between polyester satin and a calico backing. The flap has two layers of wadding. Straight stitch, satin stitch, automatic pattern and twin needle are used with the ordinary presser foot on the machine. The silver thread and sequins are stitched on by hand and the edges are bound with a bias strip.

page 29, above:
Stuffed and twin-needle quilting. This is done on a thin fabric for a greater effect. This quilting can be used on fashion pieces or for cushions (Margaret Ray).

page 29, below:
Flat, shadow work with shapes of deep coloured fabric between two thin, transparent layers. Here, zig-zag stitch is used and the top surface cut away in places (Christine Vick).

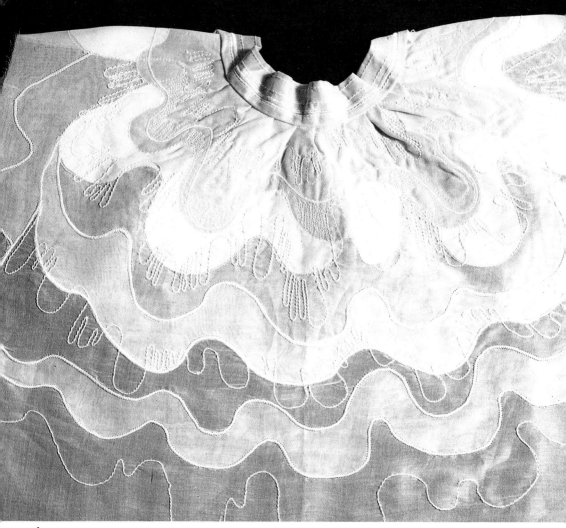

above:
Design for the front of a blouse or a sleeve. All the solid areas are enclosed between two layers of transparent fabric. One layer is cut away to give a softer, shadow effect. A straight or a zig-zag stitch holds the fabrics together. Additional wavy lines are worked over the shapes, using the darning foot and thick machine thread (Pat Phillpott).

Common machine embroidery problems

Fault	Remedy
Thread breaks regularly	The needle is blunt
Top thread misses stitches	The needle is inserted back-to-front, or not fully pushed up into the machine.
Zig-zag stitch does not pick up on both sides	Either the needle or the spool are not properly inserted, or the top thread and spool thread are different.
Stitches missed on a knitted, stretchy fabric	Either use a ball-point needle, or put tissue paper under the fabric. Use a low gear if you have one and work as slowly as possible.
Thread rucks underneath	Either you are not holding the two top thread ends when you start stitching (see page 4), or the spool is not inserted or threaded correctly, or the needle is not threaded properly.

Points to remember

Your machine must be serviced regularly.
Never force the machine if it jams, or you will strain the motor. Try to lift the needle first. If you are unable to do this, unscrew the plate that holds the spool case in position, remove the spool case, lift the needle, clear the blockage and replace.
Always keep the area around the spool free from fluff.
Always cover the machine and keep it in a warm place if possible.

Always use the machine in a warm room and put it there a day before use.
Oil your machine occasionally, after you have completed a piece of work rather than before. One or two drops of oil at each lubrication point, are enough. Wipe away any excess oil to avoid getting any on your embroidery.

Twin needle sample.
This shows a good use of the twin needle to create an additional fabric, as there is insufficient for the garment (Anne Ralphs).

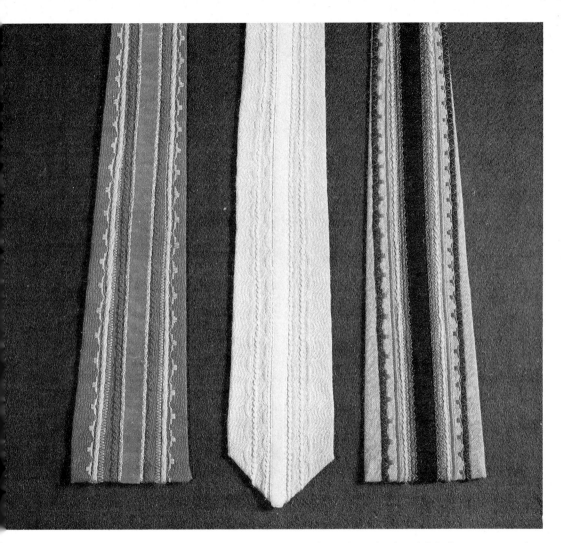

he three ties illustrate combinations of simple stitches. Satin
*itch and automatic patterns in Sylko no. 40 thread, and thick
*ool couched on top are all used. A straight stitch is used with

wool on the spool, passing through hole C to prevent excessive
looseness.

Acknowledgements

Series editor Kit Pyman

Text and drawings by Pat Phillpott

Photographs by Search Press Studios

Text, illustrations, arrangement and typography copyright © Search Press Limited 1980

First published in Great Britain in 1980 by Search Press Limited, 2–10 Jerdan Place, London SW6 5PT.

ISBN 0 85532 429 5

Made and printed in England by Burgess & Son (Abingdon) Ltd

Front cover;
The front panel of a circular blouse using a printed, furnishing voile. The panel is backed with lawn. The front centre motifs are worked upside down using the darning foot, with perlé no. 8 and then no. 3 thread in the spool. All other stitching is worked with the ordinary foot, either in straight stitch or zig-zag. Both the green zig-zag and automatic pattern are worked with perlé no. 8 thread in the spool (Pat Phillpott).

Back cover:
Appliqué, zig-zag and automatic patterns.